THE**MESSAGE**

THE
MESSAGE
OF
CHRISTMAS

EUGENE H. PETERSON

NAVPRESS○.

A NavPress resource
published in alliance
with Tyndale House
Publishers, Inc.

NAVPRESS ⬧.

NavPress is the publishing ministry of The Navigators, an international Christian organization and leader in personal spiritual development. NavPress is committed to helping people grow spiritually and enjoy lives of meaning and hope through personal and group resources that are biblically rooted, culturally relevant, and highly practical.

For more information, visit www.NavPress.com.

CONTENTS

INTRODUCTION

The story of Jesus' birth has an immense progeny. Our planet fairly teems with stories and songs, paintings and drama that got their start from this story. The reproductive energies show no sign of tapering off. Writers and singers and artists, to say nothing of countless children and parents and grandparents all over the world, continue to find fresh and novel ways of keeping this story going.

But even more impressive are the lives that continue to get a fresh start—a new birth—in the story of this birth. Day after day, men and women who feel more dead than alive, in the hearing or singing or seeing of this story, rediscover the utter and unspeakable and beautiful preciousness of life. The story of Jesus' birth gets reproduced in these human lives still, over and over and over again.

The birth of Jesus is a birth with a message. It takes the entire Bible to bring the complete message, but this birth is the core of it: In Jesus, God is here to give us life, real life.

THE
MESSAGE
OF
CHRISTMAS

A SAVIOR FORETOLD

A Righteous Branch

JEREMIAH 23:5-6

"Time's coming"—God's Decree—
   "when I'll establish a truly righteous
      David-Branch,
A ruler who knows how to rule justly.
   He'll make sure of justice and keep people
      united.
In his time Judah will be secure again
   and Israel will live in safety.
This is the name they'll give him:
   'God-Who-Puts-Everything-Right.'"

A Child Will Be Born to Us

ISAIAH 9:2-7

The people who walked in darkness
   have seen a great light.
For those who lived in a land of deep
      shadows—

light! sunbursts of light!
You repopulated the nation,
    you expanded its joy.
Oh, they're so glad in your presence!
    Festival joy!
The joy of a great celebration,
    sharing rich gifts and warm
        greetings.
The abuse of oppressors and cruelty
        of tyrants—
    all their whips and cudgels and curses—
Is gone, done away with, a deliverance
    as surprising and sudden as Gideon's old
        victory over Midian.
The boots of all those invading troops,
    along with their shirts soaked with innocent
        blood,
Will be piled in a heap and burned,
    a fire that will burn for days!
For a child has been born—for us!
    the gift of a son—for us!
He'll take over
    the running of the world.
His names will be: Amazing Counselor,
    Strong God,

Eternal Father,
>   Prince of Wholeness.
His ruling authority will grow,
>   and there'll be no limits to the wholeness he
>   brings.
He'll rule from the historic David throne
>   over that promised kingdom.
He'll put that kingdom on a firm footing
>   and keep it going
With fair dealing and right living,
>   beginning now and lasting always.
The zeal of GOD-of-the-Angel-Armies
>   will do all this.

A Righteous Judge

ISAIAH 11:1-5

>   A green Shoot will sprout from Jesse's stump,
>   from his roots a budding Branch.
>   The life-giving Spirit of GOD will hover
>   over him,
>   the Spirit that brings wisdom and
>   understanding,
>   The Spirit that gives direction and builds
>   strength,

the Spirit that instills knowledge and
Fear-of-God.
Fear-of-God
will be all his joy and delight.
He won't judge by appearances,
won't decide on the basis of hearsay.
He'll judge the needy by what is right,
render decisions on earth's poor with justice.
His words will bring everyone to awed attention.
A mere breath from his lips will topple the
wicked.
Each morning he'll pull on sturdy work clothes
and boots,
and build righteousness and faithfulness in
the land.

A Suffering Servant

ISAIAH 53:1-12
Who believes what we've heard and seen?
Who would have thought God's saving
power would look like this?

The servant grew up before God—a scrawny
seedling,
a scrubby plant in a parched field.

There was nothing attractive about him,
    nothing to cause us to take a second look.
He was looked down on and passed over,
    a man who suffered, who knew pain
        firsthand.
One look at him and people turned away.
    We looked down on him, thought he
        was scum.
But the fact is, it was *our* pains he carried—
    our disfigurements, all the things wrong
        with *us*.
We thought he brought it on himself,
    that God was punishing him for his own
        failures.
But it was our sins that did that to him,
    that ripped and tore and crushed him—
        our sins!
He took the punishment, and that made us
        whole.
    Through his bruises we get healed.
We're all like sheep who've wandered off and
        gotten lost.
    We've all done our own thing, gone our
        own way.

And GOD has piled all our sins, everything
    we've done wrong,
     on him, on him.

He was beaten, he was tortured,
    but he didn't say a word.
Like a lamb taken to be slaughtered
    and like a sheep being sheared,
    he took it all in silence.
Justice miscarried, and he was led off—
    and did anyone really know what was
     happening?
He died without a thought for his own welfare,
    beaten bloody for the sins of my people.
They buried him with the wicked,
    threw him in a grave with a rich man,
Even though he'd never hurt a soul
    or said one word that wasn't true.

Still, it's what GOD had in mind all along,
    to crush him with pain.
The plan was that he give himself as an offer-
    ing for sin
    so that he'd see life come from it—life, life,
     and more life.

And GOD's plan will deeply prosper
    through him.

Out of that terrible travail of soul,
    he'll see that it's worth it and be glad he
      did it.
Through what he experienced, my righteous
      one, my servant,
    will make many "righteous ones,"
    as he himself carries the burden of their sins.
Therefore I'll reward him extravagantly—
    the best of everything, the highest honors—
Because he looked death in the face and didn't
      flinch,
    because he embraced the company of the
      lowest.
He took on his own shoulders the sin of the
      many,
    he took up the cause of all the
      black sheep.

Behold My Chosen One

ISAIAH 42:1-4
    "Take a good look at my servant.
      I'm backing him to the hilt.

He's the one I chose,
    and I couldn't be more pleased with him.
I've bathed him with my Spirit, my *life*.
    He'll set everything right among the nations.
He won't call attention to what he does
    with loud speeches or gaudy parades.
He won't brush aside the bruised and the hurt
    and he won't disregard the small and
        insignificant,
    but he'll steadily and firmly set things right.
He won't tire out and quit. He won't be
        stopped
    until he's finished his work—to set things
        right on earth.
Far-flung ocean islands
    wait expectantly for his teaching."

Your King Is Coming

ZECHARIAH 9:9-10

    "Shout and cheer, Daughter Zion!
        Raise the roof, Daughter Jerusalem!
    Your king is coming!
        a good king who makes all things right,
        a humble king riding a donkey,
        a mere colt of a donkey.

I've had it with war—no more chariots in
     Ephraim,
  no more war horses in Jerusalem,
  no more swords and spears, bows and
     arrows.
He will offer peace to the nations,
  a peaceful rule worldwide,
  from the four winds to the seven seas."

A Virgin with Child

ISAIAH 7:10-14

GOD spoke again to Ahaz. This time he said, "Ask
for a sign from your GOD. Ask anything. Be extrav-
agant. Ask for the moon!"

But Ahaz said, "I'd never do that. I'd never make
demands like that on GOD!"

So Isaiah told him, "Then listen to this, gov-
ernment of David! It's bad enough that you make
people tired with your pious, timid hypocrisies,
but now you're making God tired. So the Master
is going to give you a sign anyway. Watch for
this: A girl who is presently a virgin will get pregnant. She'll bear a son and name him Immanuel
(God-With-Us)."

The Announcement to Mary

LUKE 1:26-38

In the sixth month of Elizabeth's pregnancy, God sent the angel Gabriel to the Galilean village of Nazareth to a virgin engaged to be married to a man descended from David. His name was Joseph, and the virgin's name, Mary. Upon entering, Gabriel greeted her:

> Good morning!
> You're beautiful with God's beauty,
> Beautiful inside and out!
> God be with you.

She was thoroughly shaken, wondering what was behind a greeting like that. But the angel assured her, "Mary, you have nothing to fear. God has a surprise for you: You will become pregnant and give birth to a son and call his name Jesus.

> He will be great,
>   be called 'Son of the Highest.'
> The Lord God will give him
>   the throne of his father David;

He will rule Jacob's house forever—
    no end, ever, to his kingdom."

Mary said to the angel, "But how? I've never slept with a man."

The angel answered,

The Holy Spirit will come upon you,
    the power of the Highest hover over you;
Therefore, the child you bring to birth
    will be called Holy, Son of God.

"And did you know that your cousin Elizabeth conceived a son, old as she is? Everyone called her barren, and here she is six months pregnant! Nothing, you see, is impossible with God."

And Mary said,

Yes, I see it all now:
    I'm the Lord's maid, ready to serve.
Let it be with me
    just as you say.

Then the angel left her.

Elizabeth and Mary

LUKE 1:39-56

Mary didn't waste a minute. She got up and traveled to a town in Judah in the hill country, straight to Zachariah's house, and greeted Elizabeth. When Elizabeth heard Mary's greeting, the baby in her womb leaped. She was filled with the Holy Spirit, and sang out exuberantly,

> You're so blessed among women,
>   and the babe in your womb, also blessed!
> And why am I so blessed that
>   the mother of my Lord visits me?
> The moment the sound of your
>   greeting entered my ears,
> The babe in my womb
>   skipped like a lamb for sheer joy.
> Blessed woman, who believed what God said,
>   believed every word would come true!

And Mary said,

> I'm bursting with God-news;
>   I'm dancing the song of my Savior God.

God took one good look at me, and look what
happened—
I'm the most fortunate woman on earth!
What God has done for me will never be
forgotten,
the God whose very name is holy, set apart
from all others.
His mercy flows in wave after wave
on those who are in awe before him.
He bared his arm and showed his strength,
scattered the bluffing braggarts.
He knocked tyrants off their high horses,
pulled victims out of the mud.
The starving poor sat down to a banquet;
the callous rich were left out in the cold.
He embraced his chosen child, Israel;
he remembered and piled on the mercies,
piled them high.
It's exactly what he promised,
beginning with Abraham and right up to
now.

Mary stayed with Elizabeth for three months
and then went back to her own home.

A SAVIOR IS BORN

The Birth of Jesus

MATTHEW 1:18-25

The birth of Jesus took place like this. His mother, Mary, was engaged to be married to Joseph. Before they came to the marriage bed, Joseph discovered she was pregnant. (It was by the Holy Spirit, but he didn't know that.) Joseph, chagrined but noble, determined to take care of things quietly so Mary would not be disgraced.

While he was trying to figure a way out, he had a dream. God's angel spoke in the dream: "Joseph, son of David, don't hesitate to get married. Mary's pregnancy is Spirit-conceived. God's Holy Spirit has made her pregnant. She will bring a son to birth, and when she does, you, Joseph, will name him Jesus—'God saves'—because he will save his people from their sins." This would bring the prophet's embryonic sermon to full term:

Watch for this—a virgin will get pregnant and
    bear a son;
They will name him Immanuel (Hebrew for
    "God is with us").

Then Joseph woke up. He did exactly what
God's angel commanded in the dream: He married
Mary. But he did not consummate the marriage
until she had the baby. He named the baby Jesus.

LUKE 2:1-7
About that time Caesar Augustus ordered a census
to be taken throughout the Empire. This was the
first census when Quirinius was governor of Syria.
Everyone had to travel to his own ancestral home-
town to be accounted for. So Joseph went from
the Galilean town of Nazareth up to Bethlehem in
Judah, David's town, for the census. As a descen-
dant of David, he had to go there. He went with
Mary, his fiancée, who was pregnant.

While they were there, the time came for her to
give birth. She gave birth to a son, her firstborn.
She wrapped him in a blanket and laid him in a
manger, because there was no room in the hostel.

The Shepherds and Angels Came

LUKE 2:8-20

There were sheepherders camping in the neighborhood. They had set night watches over their sheep. Suddenly, God's angel stood among them and God's glory blazed around them. They were terrified. The angel said, "Don't be afraid. I'm here to announce a great and joyful event that is meant for everybody, worldwide: A Savior has just been born in David's town, a Savior who is Messiah and Master. This is what you're to look for: a baby wrapped in a blanket and lying in a manger."

At once the angel was joined by a huge angelic choir singing God's praises:

Glory to God in the heavenly heights,
Peace to all men and women on earth who
please him.

As the angel choir withdrew into heaven, the sheepherders talked it over. "Let's get over to Bethlehem as fast as we can and see for ourselves what God has revealed to us." They left, running, and found Mary and Joseph, and the baby lying in the manger. Seeing was believing. They told everyone they met what the angels had said about this child. All who heard the sheepherders were impressed.

Mary kept all these things to herself, holding them dear, deep within herself. The sheepherders returned and let loose, glorifying and praising God for everything they had heard and seen. It turned out exactly the way they'd been told!

Presentation in the Temple

LUKE 2:21-38

When the eighth day arrived, the day of circumcision, the child was named Jesus, the name given by the angel before he was conceived.

Then when the days stipulated by Moses for purification were complete, they took him up to Jerusalem to offer him to God as commanded in God's Law: "Every male who opens the womb shall be a holy offering to God," and also to sacrifice the "pair of doves or two young pigeons" prescribed in God's Law.

In Jerusalem at the time, there was a man, Simeon by name, a good man, a man who lived in the prayerful expectancy of help for Israel. And the Holy Spirit was on him. The Holy Spirit had

shown him that he would see the Messiah of God
before he died. Led by the Spirit, he entered the
Temple. As the parents of the child Jesus brought
him in to carry out the rituals of the Law, Simeon
took him into his arms and blessed God:

> God, you can now release your servant;
>   release me in peace as you promised.
> With my own eyes I've seen your salvation;
>   it's now out in the open for everyone to see:
> A God-revealing light to the non-Jewish
>   nations,
>   and of glory for your people Israel.

Jesus' father and mother were speechless with
surprise at these words. Simeon went on to bless
them, and said to Mary his mother,

> This child marks both the failure and
>   the recovery of many in Israel,
> A figure misunderstood and contradicted—
>   the pain of a sword-thrust through you—
> But the rejection will force honesty,
>   as God reveals who they really are.

Anna the prophetess was also there, a daughter of Phanuel from the tribe of Asher. She was by now a very old woman. She had been married seven years and a widow for eighty-four. She never left the Temple area, worshiping night and day with her fastings and prayers. At the very time Simeon was praying, she showed up, broke into an anthem of praise to God, and talked about the child to all who were waiting expectantly for the freeing of Jerusalem.

The Visit of the Magi

MATTHEW 2:1-12

After Jesus was born in Bethlehem village, Judah territory—this was during Herod's kingship—a band of scholars arrived in Jerusalem from the East. They asked around, "Where can we find and pay homage to the newborn King of the Jews? We observed a star in the eastern sky that signaled his birth. We're on pilgrimage to worship him."

When word of their inquiry got to Herod, he was terrified—and not Herod alone, but most of Jerusalem as well. Herod lost no time. He gathered all the high priests and religion scholars in the city together and asked, "Where is the Messiah supposed to be born?"

They told him, "Bethlehem, Judah territory. The prophet Micah wrote it plainly:

It's you, Bethlehem, in Judah's land,
    no longer bringing up the rear.
From you will come the leader
    who will shepherd-rule my people, my
        Israel."

Herod then arranged a secret meeting with the scholars from the East. Pretending to be as devout as they were, he got them to tell him exactly when the birth-announcement star appeared. Then he told them the prophecy about Bethlehem, and said, "Go find this child. Leave no stone unturned. As soon as you find him, send word and I'll join you at once in your worship."

Instructed by the king, they set off. Then the star appeared again, the same star they had seen in the eastern skies. It led them on until it hovered over the place of the child. They could hardly contain themselves: They were in the right place! They had arrived at the right time!

They entered the house and saw the child in the arms of Mary, his mother. Overcome, they kneeled and worshiped him. Then they opened their luggage and presented gifts: gold, frankincense, myrrh.

In a dream, they were warned not to report back to Herod. So they worked out another route, left the territory without being seen, and returned to their own country.

God in the Neighborhood

JOHN 1:1-5, 9-14

> The Word was first,
>> the Word present to God,
>> God present to the Word.
> The Word was God,
>> in readiness for God from day one.
>
> Everything was created through him;
>> nothing—not one thing!—
>> came into being without him.
> What came into existence was Life,
>> and the Life was Light to live by.
> The Life-Light blazed out of the darkness;
>> the darkness couldn't put it out. . . .

The Life-Light was the real thing:
  Every person entering Life
  he brings into Light.
He was in the world,
  the world was there through him,
  and yet the world didn't even notice.
He came to his own people,
  but they didn't want him.
But whoever did want him,
  who believed he was who he claimed
  and would do what he said,
He made to be their true selves,
  their child-of-God selves.
These are the God-begotten,
  not blood-begotten,
  not flesh-begotten,
  not sex-begotten.

The Word became flesh and blood,
  and moved into the neighborhood.
We saw the glory with our own eyes,
  the one-of-a-kind glory,
  like Father, like Son,
Generous inside and out,
  true from start to finish.

A SAVIOR LIVES ON

The Humility of Christ

PHILIPPIANS 2:5-11

Think of yourselves the way Christ Jesus thought of himself. He had equal status with God but didn't think so much of himself that he had to cling to the advantages of that status no matter what. Not at all. When the time came, he set aside the privileges of deity and took on the status of a slave, became *human*! Having become human, he stayed human. It was an incredibly humbling process. He didn't claim special privileges. Instead, he lived a selfless, obedient life and then died a selfless, obedient death—and the worst kind of death at that—a crucifixion.

Because of that obedience, God lifted him high and honored him far beyond anyone or anything, ever, so that all created beings in heaven and on earth—even those long ago dead and buried—will bow in worship before this Jesus Christ, and call out in praise that he is the Master of all, to the glorious honor of God the Father.

The Preeminent Christ

COLOSSIANS 1:15-23

We look at this Son and see the God who cannot be seen. We look at this Son and see God's original purpose in everything created. For everything, absolutely everything, above and below, visible and invisible, rank after rank after rank of angels—*everything* got started in him and finds its purpose in him. He was there before any of it came into existence and holds it all together right up to this moment. And when it comes to the church, he organizes and holds it together, like a head does a body.

He was supreme in the beginning and—leading the resurrection parade—he is supreme in the end. From beginning to end he's there, towering far above everything, everyone. So spacious is he, so roomy, that everything of God finds its proper place in him without crowding. Not only that, but all the broken and dislocated pieces of the universe—people and things, animals and atoms—get properly fixed and fit together in vibrant harmonies, all because of his death, his blood that poured down from the cross.

You yourselves are a case study of what he does. At one time you all had your backs turned to God, thinking rebellious thoughts of him, giving him trouble every chance you got. But now, by giving himself completely at the Cross, actually *dying* for you, Christ brought you over to God's side and put your lives together, whole and holy in his presence. You don't walk away from a gift like that! You stay grounded and steady in that bond of trust, constantly tuned in to the Message, careful not to be distracted or diverted. There is no other Message—just this one. Every creature under heaven gets this same Message. I, Paul, am a messenger of this Message.

Worthy Is the Lamb

REVELATION 5:1-14

I saw a scroll in the right hand of the One Seated on the Throne. It was written on both sides, fastened with seven seals. I also saw a powerful Angel, calling out in a voice like thunder, "Is there anyone who can open the scroll, who can break its seals?"

There was no one—no one in Heaven, no one on earth, no one from the underworld—able to break open the scroll and read it.

I wept and wept and wept that no one was found

able to open the scroll, able to read it. One of the Elders said, "Don't weep. Look—the Lion from Tribe Judah, the Root of David's Tree, has conquered. He can open the scroll, can rip through the seven seals."

So I looked, and there, surrounded by Throne, Animals, and Elders, was a Lamb, slaughtered but standing tall. Seven horns he had, and seven eyes, the Seven Spirits of God sent into all the earth. He came to the One Seated on the Throne and took the scroll from his right hand. The moment he took the scroll, the Four Animals and Twenty-four Elders fell down and worshiped the Lamb. Each had a harp and each had a bowl, a gold bowl filled with incense, the prayers of God's holy people. And they sang a new song:

> Worthy! Take the scroll, open its seals.
> Slain! Paying in blood, you bought men and
> women,
> Bought them back from all over the earth,
> Bought them back for God.
> Then you made them a Kingdom, Priests for
> our God,
> Priest-kings to rule over the earth.

I looked again. I heard a company of Angels around the Throne, the Animals, and the Elders—ten thousand times ten thousand their number, thousand after thousand after thousand in full song:

> The slain Lamb is worthy!
> Take the power, the wealth, the wisdom, the
>   strength!
> Take the honor, the glory, the blessing!

Then I heard every creature in Heaven and earth, in underworld and sea, join in, all voices in all places, singing:

> To the One on the Throne! To the Lamb!
> The blessing, the honor, the glory, the strength,
> For age after age after age.

The Four Animals called out, "Oh, Yes!" The Elders fell to their knees and worshiped.

The New Heaven and New Earth

REVELATION 21:1-7

I saw Heaven and earth new-created. Gone the first Heaven, gone the first earth, gone the sea.

I saw Holy Jerusalem, new-created, descending resplendent out of Heaven, as ready for God as a bride for her husband.

I heard a voice thunder from the Throne: "Look! Look! God has moved into the neighborhood, making his home with men and women! They're his people, he's their God. He'll wipe every tear from their eyes. Death is gone for good—tears gone, crying gone, pain gone—all the first order of things gone." The Enthroned continued, "Look! I'm making everything new. Write it all down—each word dependable and accurate."

Then he said, "It's happened. I'm A to Z. I'm the Beginning, I'm the Conclusion. From Water-of-Life Well I give freely to the thirsty. Conquerors inherit all this. I'll be God to them, they'll be sons and daughters to me."

THE
GIFTS
OF
CHRISTMAS

UNWRAP THE GIFTS

As we open and receive the gift of God's Son—first given at Christmas—we find other gifts hidden in the package. Through Jesus, we experience God's unconditional love and the power to gift that love to others. As God fills our lives with his presence, we find his joy, peace, and hope welling up within, no matter what our circumstances. Our lives, once empty and aimless, are filled with God's purpose and calling. We experience real forgiveness—no matter what our past. And we begin to find the strength and freedom to forgive.

Now claim these gifts for yourselves—then pass them on.

LOVE

At Christmas, God demonstrated his love for us by sending his Son to be born as a human baby—to live among us and ultimately die for us. As we receive God's love and are transformed by it, we are called in turn to love God by loving others as his representatives in this broken world.

JOHN 3:16-18

[Jesus said,] "This is how much God loved the world: He gave his Son, his one and only Son. And this is why: so that no one need be destroyed; by believing in him, anyone can have a whole and lasting life. God didn't go to all the trouble of sending his Son merely to point an accusing finger, telling the world how bad it was. He came to help, to put the world right again. Anyone who trusts in him is acquitted; anyone who refuses to trust him has long since been under the death sentence without knowing it. And why? Because of that person's failure to believe in the one-of-a-kind Son of God when introduced to him."

1 JOHN 4:7-12

My beloved friends, let us continue to love each

other since love comes from God. Everyone who loves is born of God and experiences a relationship with God. The person who refuses to love doesn't know the first thing about God, because God *is* love—so you can't know him if you don't love. This is how God showed his love for us: God sent his only Son into the world so we might live through him. This is the kind of love we are talking about—not that we once upon a time loved God, but that he loved us and sent his Son as a sacrifice to clear away our sins and the damage they've done to our relationship with God.

My dear, dear friends, if God loved us like this, we certainly ought to love each other. No one has seen God, ever. But if we love one another, God dwells deeply within us, and his love becomes complete in us—perfect love!

1 CORINTHIANS 13:1-13

If I speak with human eloquence and angelic ecstasy but don't love, I'm nothing but the creaking of a rusty gate.

If I speak God's Word with power, revealing all his mysteries and making everything plain as day,

and if I have faith that says to a mountain, "Jump,"
and it jumps, but I don't love, I'm nothing.

If I give everything I own to the poor and even
go to the stake to be burned as a martyr, but I don't
love, I've gotten nowhere. So, no matter what I say,
what I believe, and what I do, I'm bankrupt without love.

Love never gives up.
Love cares more for others than for self.
Love doesn't want what it doesn't have.
Love doesn't strut,
Doesn't have a swelled head,
Doesn't force itself on others,
Isn't always "me first,"
Doesn't fly off the handle,
Doesn't keep score of the sins of others,
Doesn't revel when others grovel,
Takes pleasure in the flowering of truth,
Puts up with anything,
Trusts God always,
Always looks for the best,
Never looks back,
But keeps going to the end.

Love never dies. Inspired speech will be over some day; praying in tongues will end; understanding will reach its limit. We know only a portion of the truth, and what we say about God is always incomplete. But when the Complete arrives, our incompletes will be canceled.

When I was an infant at my mother's breast, I gurgled and cooed like any infant. When I grew up, I left those infant ways for good.

We don't yet see things clearly. We're squinting in a fog, peering through a mist. But it won't be long before the weather clears and the sun shines bright! We'll see it all then, see it all as clearly as God sees us, knowing him directly just as he knows us!

But for right now, until that completeness, we have three things to do to lead us toward that consummation: Trust steadily in God, hope unswervingly, love extravagantly. And the best of the three is love.

JOY

The angels announced to the shepherds that the coming of Jesus was a great and joyful event that was significant for everyone. God had come to live among us! Life in this world is often difficult, but living with God's constant presence and an eternal hope allows us to experience joy no matter what we may face. God's presence in our lives is always a reason for joy.

HABAKKUK 3:17-19

Though the cherry trees don't blossom
and the strawberries don't ripen,
Though the apples are worm-eaten
and the wheat fields stunted,
Though the sheep pens are sheepless
and the cattle barns empty,
I'm singing joyful praise to GOD.
I'm turning cartwheels of joy to my Savior
God.
Counting on GOD's Rule to prevail,
I take heart and gain strength.
I run like a deer.
I feel like I'm king of the mountain!

PHILIPPIANS 4:4-7

Celebrate God all day, every day. I mean, *revel* in him! Make it as clear as you can to all you meet that you're on their side, working with them and not against them. Help them see that the Master is about to arrive. He could show up any minute!

Don't fret or worry. Instead of worrying, pray. Let petitions and praises shape your worries into prayers, letting God know your concerns. Before you know it, a sense of God's wholeness, everything coming together for good, will come and settle you down. It's wonderful what happens when Christ displaces worry at the center of your life.

1 PETER 4:7-11

Everything in the world is about to be wrapped up, so take nothing for granted. Stay wide-awake in prayer. Most of all, love each other as if your life depended on it. Love makes up for practically anything. Be quick to give a meal to the hungry, a bed to the homeless—cheerfully. Be generous with the different things God gave you, passing them around so all get in on it: if words, let it be God's words; if help, let it be God's hearty help. That way, God's bright presence will be evident in everything

through Jesus, and *he'll* get all the credit as the One
mighty in everything—encores to the end of time.
Oh, yes!

PEACE

The prophet Isaiah spoke of the Messiah as the Prince of Wholeness—the Prince of Peace—and so we often reflect on peace and wholeness as a gift of Christmas. In a world filled with conflict, anxiety, loneliness, and suffering, so many of us long for peace—to be complete and whole. Jesus offers us personal wholeness and peace with God and his people through his first coming, and we now long for the ultimate eternal wholeness he will bring when he returns.

MATTHEW 11:27-30

Jesus resumed talking to the people, but now tenderly. "The Father has given me all these things to do and say. This is a unique Father-Son operation, coming out of Father and Son intimacies and knowledge. No one knows the Son the way the Father does, nor the Father the way the Son does. But I'm not keeping it to myself; I'm ready to go over it line by line with anyone willing to listen.

"Are you tired? Worn out? Burned out on religion? Come to me. Get away with me and you'll recover your life. I'll show you how to take a real rest. Walk with me and work with me—watch how I do it. Learn the unforced rhythms of grace. I won't lay anything heavy or ill-fitting on you. Keep company with me and you'll learn to live freely and lightly."

JOHN 14:25-27

[Jesus said,] "I'm telling you these things while I'm still living with you. The Friend, the Holy Spirit whom the Father will send at my request, will make everything plain to you. He will remind you of all the things I have told you. I'm leaving you well and whole. That's my parting gift to you. Peace. I don't leave you the way you're used to being left—feeling abandoned, bereft. So don't be upset. Don't be distraught."

COLOSSIANS 3:15-17

Let the peace of Christ keep you in tune with each other, in step with each other. None of this going off and doing your own thing. And cultivate thankfulness. Let the Word of Christ—the Message—have the run of the house. Give it plenty of room in your lives. Instruct and direct one another using good common sense. And sing, sing your hearts out to God! Let every detail in your lives—words, actions, whatever—be done in the name of the Master, Jesus, thanking God the Father every step of the way.

HOPE

In a world filled with conflict and suffering, people often lose all hope. The coming of Jesus into this world offers us a clear and real hope that everything wrong in the world will be made right again in the end. And by following Jesus, we can offer hope to others not only for life today but also for the eternal life to come.

HEBREWS 12:1-13

Do you see what this means—all these pioneers who blazed the way, all these veterans cheering us on? It means we'd better get on with it. Strip down, start running—and never quit! No extra spiritual fat, no parasitic sins. Keep your eyes on *Jesus*, who both began and finished this race we're in. Study how he did it. Because he never lost sight of where he was headed—that exhilarating finish in and with God—he could put up with anything along the way: Cross, shame, whatever. And now he's *there*, in the place of honor, right alongside God. When you find yourselves flagging in your faith, go over that story again, item by item, that long litany of hostility he plowed through. *That* will shoot adrenaline into your souls!

In this all-out match against sin, others have suffered far worse than you, to say nothing of what Jesus went through—all that bloodshed! So don't feel sorry for yourselves. Or have you forgotten how good parents treat children, and that God regards you as *his* children?

My dear child, don't shrug off God's discipline,
    but don't be crushed by it either.
It's the child he loves that he disciplines;
    the child he embraces, he also corrects.

God is educating you; that's why you must never drop out. He's treating you as dear children. This trouble you're in isn't punishment; it's *training*, the normal experience of children. Only irresponsible parents leave children to fend for themselves. Would you prefer an irresponsible God? We respect our own parents for training and not spoiling us, so why not embrace God's training so we can truly *live*? While we were children, our parents did what *seemed* best to them. But God is doing what *is* best for us, training us to live God's holy best. At the time, discipline isn't much fun. It always feels like it's going against the grain. Later, of course, it pays off handsomely, for it's the well-trained who find themselves mature in their relationship with God.

So don't sit around on your hands! No more dragging your feet! Clear the path for long-distance runners so no one will trip and fall, so no one will step in a hole and sprain an ankle. Help each other out. And run for it!

JAMES 1:2-18

Consider it a sheer gift, friends, when tests and challenges come at you from all sides. You know that under pressure, your faith-life is forced into the open and shows its true colors. So don't try to get out of anything prematurely. Let it do its work so you become mature and well-developed, not deficient in any way.

If you don't know what you're doing, pray to the Father. He loves to help. You'll get his help, and won't be condescended to when you ask for it. Ask boldly, believingly, without a second thought. People who "worry their prayers" are like wind-whipped waves. Don't think you're going to get anything from the Master that way, adrift at sea, keeping all your options open.

When down-and-outers get a break, cheer! And

when the arrogant rich are brought down to size, cheer! Prosperity is as short-lived as a wildflower, so don't ever count on it. You know that as soon as the sun rises, pouring down its scorching heat, the flower withers. Its petals wilt and, before you know it, that beautiful face is a barren stem. Well, that's a picture of the "prosperous life." At the very moment everyone is looking on in admiration, it fades away to nothing.

Anyone who meets a testing challenge head-on and manages to stick it out is mighty fortunate. For such persons loyally in love with God, the reward is life and more life.

Don't let anyone under pressure to give in to evil say, "God is trying to trip me up." God is impervious to evil, and puts evil in no one's way. The temptation to give in to evil comes from us and only us. We have no one to blame but the leering, seducing flare-up of our own lust. Lust gets pregnant, and has a baby: sin! Sin grows up to adulthood, and becomes a real killer.

So, my very dear friends, don't get thrown off course. Every desirable and beneficial gift comes out of heaven. The gifts are rivers of light cascading down from the Father of Light. There is nothing deceitful in God, nothing two-faced, nothing fickle. He brought us to life using the true Word, showing us off as the crown of all his creatures.

1 PETER 4:12-19

Friends, when life gets really difficult, don't jump to the conclusion that God isn't on the job. Instead, be glad that you are in the very thick of what Christ experienced. This is a spiritual refining process, with glory just around the corner.

If you're abused because of Christ, count yourself fortunate. It's the Spirit of God and his glory in you that brought you to the notice of others. If they're on you because you broke the law or disturbed the peace, that's a different matter. But if it's because you're a Christian, don't give it a second thought. Be proud of the distinguished status reflected in that name!

It's judgment time for God's own family. We're first in line. If it starts with us, think what it's going to be like for those who refuse God's Message!

If good people barely make it,
What's in store for the bad?

So if you find life difficult because you're doing what God said, take it in stride. Trust him. He knows what he's doing, and he'll keep on doing it.

PURPOSE

By sending his Son at Christmas to reconcile us to himself, God demonstrated his desire to reach out to us and to call us into friendship with himself through Jesus. Our purpose in life is first to joyfully embrace this friendship with God, and then to join God in his redeeming work in the world, whatever form that might take.

EPHESIANS 2:7-10

Now God has us where he wants us, with all the time in this world and the next to shower grace and kindness upon us in Christ Jesus. Saving is all his idea, and all his work. All we do is trust him enough to let him do it. It's God's gift from start to finish! We don't play the major role. If we did, we'd probably go around bragging that we'd done the whole thing! No, we neither make nor save ourselves. God does both the making and saving. He creates each of us by Christ Jesus to join him in the work he does, the good work he has gotten ready for us to do, work we had better be doing.

ROMANS 8:15-25

This resurrection life you received from God is not a timid, grave-tending life. It's adventurously expectant, greeting God with a childlike "What's next, Papa?" God's Spirit touches our spirits and confirms who we really are. We know who he is, and we know who we are: Father and children. And we know we are going to get what's coming to us—an unbelievable inheritance! We go through exactly what Christ goes through. If we go through the hard times with him, then we're certainly going to go through the good times with him!

That's why I don't think there's any comparison between the present hard times and the coming good times. The created world itself can hardly wait for what's coming next. Everything in creation is being more or less held back. God reins it in until both creation and all the creatures are ready and can be released at the same moment into the glorious times ahead. Meanwhile, the joyful anticipation deepens.

All around us we observe a pregnant creation. The difficult times of pain throughout the world are simply birth pangs. But it's not only around us; it's *within* us. The Spirit of God is arousing us within. We're also feeling the birth pangs. These sterile and barren bodies of ours are yearning for full deliverance. That is why waiting does not diminish us, any more than waiting diminishes a pregnant mother. We are enlarged in the waiting. We, of course, don't see what is enlarging us. But the longer we wait, the larger we become, and the more joyful our expectancy.

PHILIPPIANS 1:22-26

As long as I'm alive in this body, there is good work for me to do. If I had to choose right now, I hardly know which I'd choose. Hard choice! The desire to break camp here and be with Christ is powerful. Some days I can think of nothing better. But most days, because of what you are going through, I am sure that it's better for me to stick it out here. So I plan to be around awhile, companion to you as your growth and joy in this life of trusting God continues. You can start looking forward to a great reunion when I come visit you again. We'll be praising Christ, enjoying each other.

FORGIVENESS

By sending Jesus at Christmas, God was putting into action his plan for our forgiveness and redemption. Through his death on the cross, Jesus would pay for our guilt before God and pave the way to our reconciliation with him. And as those who have been forgiven, we are called upon to give forgiveness to all those who have wronged us.

1 JOHN 1:8-10

If we claim that we're free of sin, we're only fooling ourselves. A claim like that is errant nonsense. On the other hand, if we admit our sins—make a clean breast of them—he won't let us down; he'll be true to himself. He'll forgive our sins and purge us of all wrongdoing. If we claim that we've never sinned, we out-and-out contradict God—make a liar out of him. A claim like that only shows off our ignorance of God.

COLOSSIANS 3:12-14

So, chosen by God for this new life of love, dress in the wardrobe God picked out for you: compassion, kindness, humility, quiet strength, discipline. Be

even-tempered, content with second place, quick to forgive an offense. Forgive as quickly and completely as the Master forgave you. And regardless of what else you put on, wear love. It's your basic, all-purpose garment. Never be without it.

MATTHEW 18:21-35

Peter got up the nerve to ask, "Master, how many times do I forgive a brother or sister who hurts me? Seven?"

Jesus replied, "Seven! Hardly. Try seventy times seven.

"The kingdom of God is like a king who decided to square accounts with his servants. As he got under way, one servant was brought before him who had run up a debt of a hundred thousand dollars. He couldn't pay up, so the king ordered the man, along with his wife, children, and goods, to be auctioned off at the slave market.

"The poor wretch threw himself at the king's feet and begged, 'Give me a chance and I'll pay it all back.' Touched by his plea, the king let him off, erasing the debt.

"The servant was no sooner out of the room when he came upon one of his fellow servants who owed him ten dollars. He seized him by the throat and demanded, 'Pay up. Now!'

"The poor wretch threw himself down and begged, 'Give me a chance and I'll pay it all back.' But he wouldn't do it. He had him arrested and put in jail until the debt was paid. When the other servants saw this going on, they were outraged and brought a detailed report to the king.

"The king summoned the man and said, 'You evil servant! I forgave your entire debt when you begged me for mercy. Shouldn't you be compelled to be merciful to your fellow servant who asked for mercy?' The king was furious and put the screws to the man until he paid back his entire debt. And that's exactly what my Father in heaven is going to do to each one of you who doesn't forgive unconditionally anyone who asks for mercy."

HOW WE CAN KNOW GOD

So What's Missing?

Purpose, meaning, a reason for living—these are all things we desire and search for in life. But despite our search, we still feel empty and unfulfilled. We each have an empty place in our heart, a spiritual void, a "God-shaped vacuum." Possessions won't fill it, nor will success, relationships, or even religion. Only through a vibrant relationship with God can this void be filled. And God is reaching out to us and longs for such a relationship with us. At Christmas, he sent his Son to be born as a human baby—to reach out to us, to do everything necessary to make a relationship with God possible. But before such a relationship can be established, we need to face a serious problem.

The Problem: Sin

"The heart is hopelessly dark and deceitful, a puzzle that no one can figure out. But I, GOD, search the heart and examine the mind. I get to the heart of the human. I get to the root of things. I treat them as they really are, not as they pretend to be" (Jeremiah 17:9-10).

God's message reveals that the underlying problem is sin. Sin is not just the bad things we do, but an inherent part of who we are. We are not sinners because we sin; we sin because we are sinners. King David once said to God, "I've been out of step with you for a long time, in the wrong since before I was born" (Psalm 51:5). Since we are born sinners, sinning comes to us naturally. And every problem we experience in society today can be traced back to our refusal to do things God's way.

The Solution: Jesus

"The God-setting-things-right that we read about has become Jesus-setting-things-right for us. And not only for us, but for everyone who believes in him. For there is no difference between us and them in this. Since we've compiled this long and sorry record as sinners (both us and them) and proved that we are utterly incapable of living the glorious lives God wills for us, God did it for us" (Romans 3:22-23).

God understood our problem and knew we couldn't beat it alone. So he sent his own Son, Jesus Christ, to bridge the chasm of sin that separates us from God. Jesus laid aside his divine privileges and walked the earth as a man, experiencing all the troubles and emotions that we do. Then he was arrested on false charges and killed on a Roman cross. But this was no accident. He did it to suffer the punishment deserved by us all. And then three days later, Jesus rose from the dead, conquering sin and death forever!

The Response: Accepting God's Offer

"Now it's time to change your ways! Turn to face God so he can wipe away your sins, pour out showers of blessing to refresh you, and send you the Messiah he prepared for you, namely, Jesus" (Acts 3:19).

To know Jesus personally and have our sins forgiven, we must believe that we are sinners separated from God and that our only hope is Jesus the Messiah, the Son of God, who came and died for our sins. But we must not stop with this realization. We also need to take steps toward confessing and turning from our sins. And we must welcome Jesus Christ into our life as Lord and Savior. He will move in and help us to change from the inside out.

If you are ready to turn from your sins and believe in Jesus so you can receive God's forgiveness, take a moment to pray like this:

> *God, I'm sorry for my sins. Right now, I turn from my sins and ask you to forgive me. Thank you for sending Jesus to be born as a human baby and to die on the cross for my sins. Jesus, I ask you to come into my life and be my Lord, Savior, and Friend. Thank you for forgiving me and giving me eternal life. In the name of Jesus I pray. Amen.*

If you prayed this prayer and meant it, you can be sure that God has forgiven you and adopted you into his family.

Get the rest of
The Message

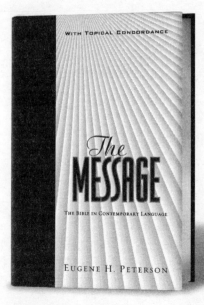

ISBN 978-1-61521-107-4